EXAMINING
OIL SPILLS

BY ANNA DALTON

CLARA
HOUSE
BOOKS

First published in 2015 by Clara House Books, an imprint of
The Oliver Press, Inc.

Clara House Books
5707 West 36th Street
Minneapolis, MN 55416
USA

Editors: Mirella Miller and Arnold Ringstad
Series Designer: Maggie Villaume

Library of Congress Cataloging-in-Publication Data

Dalton, Anna, author.
  Examining oil spills / by Anna Dalton.
      pages cm. – (Examining disasters)
  Audience: Grades 7 to 8.
  Includes an index.
  ISBN 978-1-934545-65-2 (hardcover : alk. paper) – ISBN 978-1-934545-81-2 (ebook)
  1. Oil spills–Environmental aspects–Juvenile literature. 2. Oil spills–Prevention–Juvenile
literature. 3. Oil spills–Cleanup–Juvenile literature. 4. Petroleum industry and trade–Safety
measures–Juvenile literature. I. Title.

  TD427.P4D35 2015
  363.738'2–dc23

                                        2014044474

Printed in the United States of America
CG1022015

www.oliverpress.com

CONTENTS

ONE

DERAILMENT IN QUEBEC

It was approximately 11:05 p.m. on July 5, 2013, in Nantes, Quebec, Canada. Train engineer Thomas Harding brought the train called Montreal, Main, and Atlantic (MMA) 2 to a stop. MMA 2 was carrying 72 cars full of crude oil. One of the train's locomotives had been giving Harding trouble that day. Now it was spewing oil.

Harding had turned on the train's two air brakes and manually set seven hand brakes. MMA 2's guidelines call for at least nine hand brakes to be set on trains with 70 to 79 cars. Harding left the leaking locomotive running unattended. The engine was supplying energy to the train's air brakes. MMA trains were often

Train cars piled up after leaving the track in Lac-Mégantic, Quebec, in 2013.

HORIZONTAL DRILLING AND HYDRAULIC FRACTURING

Horizontal drilling and hydraulic fracturing, or fracking, have caused a boom in oil production in recent years. Oil engineers first drill down and then horizontally into the rock where oil and gas are trapped. Next, they pump a mixture of water, sand, and chemicals into the hole. The rock fractures, or cracks, release oil and gas. Fracking and horizontal drilling can recover oil that could not be recovered otherwise, and the process allows workers to access oil under sensitive areas without disturbing the land above. However, the new methods are not without risks. If chemicals or oil get into the water supply, people may become sick.

left unattended overnight in Nantes. With the brakes set, Harding went to a hotel for the night.

After 11:00 p.m., a fire started burning in the distressed locomotive. Nantes firefighters rushed to shut off the engine to fight the blaze, but turning off the engine also meant shutting off the train's air brakes. Now, only the seven hand brakes were keeping MMA 2 from rolling 8 miles (13 km) down the hill from Nantes to the nearby town of Lac-Mégantic.

After the fire was controlled, the firefighters and MMA employees left the train unattended again. Then, the MMA 2 train began to roll down the hill toward Lac-Mégantic. It picked up speed as it went, and by the time it reached Lac-Mégantic, the train

The fires from the train derailment could not be fully extinguished for nearly two days.

was traveling an estimated 60 miles (100 km) per hour. The speed limit for that area of train track was 10 miles (16 km) per hour. Sparks shot from the train's wheels as it screeched and roared down the track.

The train went off the tracks sometime between midnight and 1:14 a.m. on July 6, 2013. Five or six explosions sounded throughout the city, and a giant fireball erupted over downtown. People felt the intense heat from the blast more than 1 mile (1.6 km) away.

Toxic fumes filled the air in the days following the accident.

AFTERMATH OF THE CRASH

Forty-seven people died in the explosions and fires from the MMA 2 train. Approximately 115 businesses were destroyed.

Sixty-three of the train's cars carrying oil exploded and spilled their contents. A toxic component of oil, called benzene, soaked into the ground. Poisonous vapors threatened the health of response workers and residents. Between 2.3 million and 3.2 million cubic feet (64,000–92,000 cubic meters) of contaminated soil had to be removed or treated. Approximately 26,000 gallons (100,000 L) of oil leaked into the nearby Chaudière River. Even more spilled into Lac Mégantic. The lake's water contained nearly 400,000 times the rate of toxins considered safe for surface water, per provincial government standards.

PIPELINE CAPACITY

Railways are only one method of transporting oil. It is quicker and cheaper to move oil through pipelines than by any other method. In the United States and Canada, 70 percent of petroleum products move through pipelines. Another 23 percent of oil moves on ships, while 4 percent moves on trucks. Only 3 percent moves by train, but that number is increasing. There are not enough pipelines to move all the oil coming out of the ground.

Cleanup of Lac-Mégantic is expected to take years and will cost hundreds of millions of dollars.

The Lac-Mégantic derailment was one of the deadliest railway disasters in history. The oil spill caused by the derailment was an environmental catastrophe. Nearly

1.6 million gallons (6 million L) of crude oil spilled into the land and water. Much of the oil remains beneath the water's surface and in the soil. It will threaten the health of people, plants, and animals for years to come.

TWO

WHAT IS OIL?

Oil is a thick, black liquid that comes from the ground and is used to make many different products. Oil pumped from the ground or the seafloor is called crude oil. It is formed from the remains of prehistoric plants and animals that settled on the bottoms of lakes, swamps, and oceans. Over long periods of time, sediment covered these remains until they were eventually buried under layers of rock. Over millions of years, the remains were exposed to heat and pressure, changing them into crude oil. Crude oil is often called petroleum or oil.

Oil is not a single chemical. It is a mixture of many chemicals called hydrocarbons. Crude oil ranges in density from light to heavy. Some types are more viscous, or resistant to flow, than others.

The oil we use for everyday energy needs comes from organisms that lived millions of years ago.

Oil can be black, dark brown, or even shades of red, orange, or yellow in color.

CONSUMPTION AND PRODUCTION

In 2012, the United States consumed more than 795 million gallons (3 billion L) of petroleum products each day. That amount is more than 500 times the volume spilled in the Lac-Mégantic disaster.

Nearly 100 countries produce crude oil. In 2012, Saudi Arabia produced the most, followed by Russia, the United States, China, and Canada. Texas, North Dakota, Alaska, California, and Oklahoma produce the most oil in the United States.

OIL PIPELINES

Oil reservoirs are often located far from refineries. Refineries are facilities in which crude oil is refined, or processed, and turned

PETROLEUM SEEPS

A petroleum seep is a place where oil or natural gas wells up from the earth's surface. Petroleum escapes through cracks and fissures in rocks and seeps out under low pressure. Ancient people took advantage of petroleum seeps. They used oil to dress wounds and for other medicinal purposes. They also used petroleum products in warfare. Petroleum seeps provide raw material for products, such as asphalt and tar, too.

Americans use oil more than any other energy source.

into petroleum products, such as gasoline for cars. To get the oil from its reservoir to a refinery, giant tanker ships carry oil across oceans. Vast pipeline networks move oil across land and water. Smaller amounts of petroleum products are shipped on trains, trucks, and barges.

Refineries are often huge, complicated structures.

Large volumes of oil are on the move every day, and most oil spills occur during transportation. But oil spills also happen during extraction, when something goes wrong drilling down to the oil reservoir or pumping the oil out.

An oil spill is any accidental release of oil or petroleum products into the environment. People make mistakes, mechanical equipment fails, and sometimes natural disasters can damage pipelines, storage tanks, or drilling rigs.

HOW SCIENCE WORKS
TANKER TRUCKS

Tanker trucks started appearing in Europe and the United States in the early 1900s. These vehicles transport petroleum products. Railroads could carry oil from the oil fields and refineries, but there were no tracks that traveled to the gas stations where automobiles could fill up. Oil companies solved this problem with tanker trucks that could carry refined petroleum products along roads. Before the motorized vehicles, oil had been transported in horse-drawn wagons.

In the next decades, tanks and vehicles improved. Tanks were built using welding instead of riveting to create a better seal and protect against leaks. Now tanker trucks are made of a variety of materials, including aluminum, steel, and plastics. Scientists and engineers are always working to make tanker trucks as safe and efficient as possible.

THREE

WHAT CAUSES AN OIL SPILL?

Oil is sometimes found in extreme locations. There is oil deep underwater and in cold Arctic regions. These problematic locations, along with the chemical properties of oil, can make working with oil dangerous. Higher risks based on location increase the chance of accidents and oil spills.

Oil forms deep underground. The deeper the reservoir is located, the greater the pore pressure, which is the pressure of fluids in a reservoir. The pore pressure is predicted before and measured throughout drilling. Drillers respond to changes in pore pressure by changing the amount and type of concrete and mud they pump into the well.

Oil companies build platforms above underwater oil reservoirs. Oil workers live and work on the platforms.

If the pressure is not kept balanced, blowouts can occur. A blowout happens when oil shoots uncontrollably out of a well. In the early days of oil drilling, blowouts were called gushers.

UNDERGROUND PRESSURE

In an oil reservoir, liquid oil fills tiny spaces in a layer of rock. The oil is trapped in the reservoir by the weight of the rock, which creates pressure in the reservoir. This force is called pore pressure. Without cement and mud in the well to balance the pore pressure, oil and gas would shoot out like soda from a shaken bottle.

DEEP-SEA DRILLING

Deep-sea drilling is more difficult than drilling on land. The oil must be retrieved through the ocean, and oil reservoirs may lie 30,000 feet (9,144 m) below the seafloor. At that depth, pore pressures can be incredibly high, reaching greater than 10,000 pounds per square inch (69 megapascals).

On April 20, 2010, the *Deepwater Horizon* oil rig blew

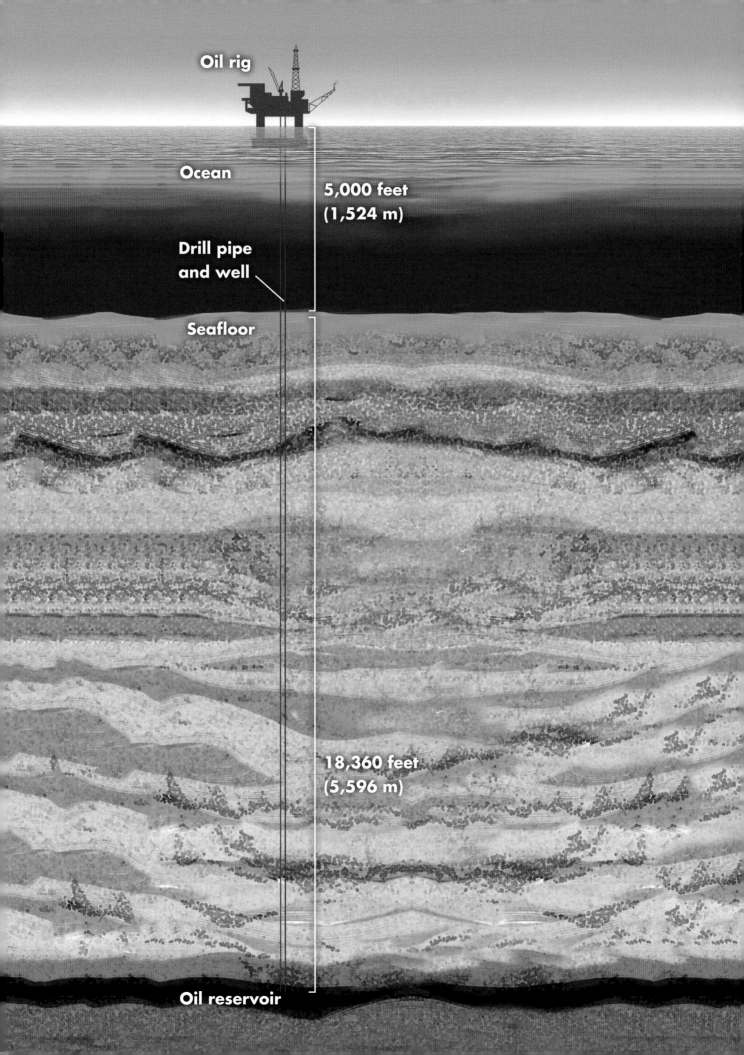

Oil rig

Ocean

5,000 feet
(1,524 m)

**Drill pipe
and well**

Seafloor

18,360 feet
(5,596 m)

Oil reservoir

Leaks from the oil well led to huge explosions on the *Deepwater Horizon*.

out in the Gulf of Mexico. Safety systems failed, and an explosion ripped through the rig. Eleven men died aboard the rig, which burned for two days before sinking. The pipe that had connected the rig to the well broke, and oil gushed into the water from the pipe. Eighty-seven days after the blowout, the leak was finally stopped.

Scientists estimate a total of 206 million gallons (780 million L) of oil were released from the well.

Some oil was recovered, but approximately 171 million gallons (647 million L) spilled into the Gulf of Mexico. It was the largest accidental offshore oil spill in history.

DANGEROUS SUBSTANCE

The risk of a blowout like the *Deepwater Horizon* oil spill is high. On the seafloor, drilling activities can disrupt temperatures and pressures. Hydrates, which develop when water mixes with another substance, are also a hazard. For example, large amounts of methane gas trapped in icy sediments could be released, causing the sediment around the well to become unstable and collapse. Hydrates can become solid when oil is exposed to high pressure and cold temperatures. They can clog well pipes.

The chemical properties of oil also make it a dangerous substance. Crude oil and petroleum products contain volatile organic compounds (VOCs). VOCs are dangerous chemicals that burn easily and often have negative health effects. Many of the VOCs in oil have a low flash point, the temperature at which a substance creates enough vapor in the air to burn. Many of the VOCs found in oil have a flash point of less than 100 degrees Fahrenheit (38°C) and are considered flammable. When there is enough vapor in the air, a spark or flame can ignite it, and the vapor will explode. If the oil contains a high concentration of VOCs, static electricity can cause an explosion. Explosions damage rigs, wells, pipelines, ships, railcars, and other oil-carrying equipment. They can also injure or kill people.

Oil also contains potentially dangerous chemicals, including sulfur and heavy metals. Over time, sulfur can weaken metal used to store and transport crude oil in a chemical process called corrosion. Rust on iron objects is a type of corrosion. Corroded areas of pipelines, storage tanks, and ships can easily leak or burst.

Engineers have developed technology to protect against these hazards and reduce the risk of oil spills. But some dangers, such as weather, are beyond their control. High winds, large waves, and lightning strikes from storms have all been responsible for tanker ship disasters.

In 2005, Hurricanes Katrina and Rita broke pipelines and damaged storage tanks in the Gulf of Mexico region. Scientists believe these hurricanes caused 11 million gallons (41.6 million L) of oil to spill.

Not all oil spills are accidents. In 1991, at the close of the Gulf War, the armed forces of Iraqi dictator Saddam Hussein blew up more than 600 Kuwaiti oil wells. Saddam was motivated to punish Kuwait, which was a major oil producer, and he

KOMI REPUBLIC PIPELINE

One of the worst pipeline spills in history occurred in the Komi Republic in Russia. The pipeline was old and had not been well maintained. The metal was badly corroded. In 1994, parts of the pipeline collapsed. More than 84 million gallons (318 million L) of oil poured onto the ground.

The fires in Kuwait burned for seven months.

also thought the smoke from the fires would protect his retreating troops from U.S.-led coalition air strikes. Toxins spewed into the air, lakes of oil formed in the desert, and more than 1 billion barrels of oil were spilled and burned.

HOW SCIENCE WORKS

During the *Deepwater Horizon* disaster, responders estimated 42,000 gallons (159,000 L) per day were leaking into the water. Later, a scientist calculated the flow rate at approximately 210,000 gallons (795,000 L) per day. This was a rough estimate, because the scientist did not know the speed of the oil leaving the well or the thickness of the oil slick on the water surface.

As satellite images and video of the leaking well became available, other scientists used new data to make their own calculations. Their estimates ranged from 850,000 gallons to 4.2 million gallons (3.2 million to 5.9 million L) per day. After the well had been closed, the official flow rates were announced. According to official reports, 2.6 million gallons (9.8 million L) per day were released on the first day of the spill. The rate decreased over the next 86 days to a final rate of 2.2 million gallons (8.4 million L) per day. The earliest estimate was based on the area of oil on the ocean surface and did not take into account underwater oil that never reached the surface. The final flow rates were based on new evidence: actual pressure measurements in the well just before the well was contained. Due to the *Deepwater Horizon* disaster, scientists now have a better understanding of how to measure the flow rate from underwater oil leaks.

FOUR

OIL SPILL IMPACTS

Oil spills cause harm to living things and the environment in many ways. When released into water, oil spreads quickly and can affect a large area. Spills on land can be absorbed into soil and enter drinking water supplies. Oil can remain in the environment at dangerous levels for years. The impacts of an oil spill can be felt far from the original leak site for years.

Crude oil can be thick and sticky. It can smother plants and small creatures. Larger aquatic animals covered in oil may drown, because oil prevents them from swimming well.

Oil is also harmful to animals in other ways. The fur of marine mammals, such as sea otters, helps them survive in cold water. Aquatic birds have

Workers try to clean up an oil-filled beach in Thailand in 2013.

water-repellent feathers. But fur and feathers coated with oil lose their ability to insulate and to shed water. Without the fur and feather protections, these animals often die from the cold.

HELPING WILDLIFE RECOVER

Wildlife biologists dug up sea turtle nests along the northern Gulf of Mexico coast following the *Deepwater Horizon* spill. They wanted to stop the turtles from swimming into oil when they hatched. Biologists also thought beach cleanup efforts might disrupt turtle nests. They uncovered the eggs and placed them in Styrofoam boxes. Scientists monitored the eggs. Once the turtles hatched, scientists released the baby turtles into the Atlantic Ocean.

When people or animals are exposed to an oil spill, they can accidentally ingest oil. Oil is toxic and causes many serious health problems. Toxic compounds found in VOCs are harmful when inhaled. These compounds may damage the brain and organs or cause cancer. Oil can also affect future generations. For example, studies have shown that fish eggs exposed to oil may not develop normally.

Even animals that do not come into direct contact with spilled oil can be affected. Zooplankton are microscopic animal organisms. In marine ecosystems, such as the Gulf of Mexico, zooplankton are

Workers attempt to clean the oil off a pelican after an oil spill in Australia in 2009.

food for other animals. Toxic compounds from spilled oil enter the bodies of zooplankton. When other animals, such as fish and shrimp, eat the zooplankton, they absorb those compounds into their bodies. If those animals are eaten by a larger creature, the compounds spread to the animal that ate them. Each time a creature eats a

EXXON VALDEZ, 25 YEARS LATER

The *Exxon Valdez* tanker spill in Alaska in 1989 was one of the worst environmental disasters of all time. It spilled approximately 11 million gallons (42 million L). Some beaches in the area still have deposits of oil today, and the oil is as toxic as the day it was spilled. The populations of many large animal species, including the sea otter, remain lower than they were before the spill. The oil in Prince William Sound, the large Alaskan bay where the *Exxon Valdez* spilled its oil, is diminishing at a rate of 0 to 4 percent each year. It will be decades or centuries before the oil is completely gone.

contaminated plant or animal, the toxic compounds are transferred, all the way up the food chain.

When oil spills in bodies of water, wind and waves can push the oil toward the shore. Important habitats such as salt marshes, mudflats, mangroves, and sandy beaches are located on shorelines. Oil can sink deep into mud and sediments and remain there for a very long time. As long as the oil persists in a habitat, the oil continues to have negative effects on plants and animals.

Coastal wetlands, such as marshes, are important habitats for fish. Marshes also help purify water and protect coasts from high storm tides. Oil kills the marsh grass. Without the grasses' root systems to hold the soil in place, tides wash

IMPACTS ON GULF BIRDS

Mississippi   Alabama   Georgia

Louisiana

Deepwater Horizon

Florida

Gulf of Mexico

IMPACTS ON GULF BIRDS
This diagram shows where dead seabirds were collected along the northern Gulf Coast after the *Deepwater Horizon* spill. Larger dots indicate a greater number of dead birds. Where were the largest numbers of dead birds found? What can you tell about the direction of the oil from the spill from this data?

away the soil, and the marshland habitat is reduced or destroyed.

The economic impacts of oil spills are enormous. After the *Deepwater Horizon* spill, fisheries and oyster grounds were closed while the wildlife was inspected. All deep-sea drilling in the Gulf of Mexico and the Pacific Ocean was temporarily banned. People stopped visiting popular tourist attractions in states bordering the Gulf of Mexico because of the oiled beaches and fears of air pollution.

Fishermen, drilling rig workers, and people in the tourism industry were unable to work. British Petroleum (BP), the company that operated *Deepwater Horizon*, set aside more than $40 billion to pay for fines, cleanup, and compensation for victims of the spill, but BP could face expenses related to the oil spill for years to come. The full extent of the economic damage from the spill is likely much higher than $40 billion. The value of ecological goods and services like lost wetlands is hard to calculate.

HOW SCIENCE WORKS
OIL SPILL MODELS

Teams of scientists work together to create computer models for oil spills. The Automated Data Inquiry for Oil Spills model estimates how the spilled oil will behave over time. These physical and chemical changes in the environment are called weathering. Another model, the General National Oceanic and Atmospheric Administration (NOAA) Operational Modeling Environment, predicts where oil will spread based on winds and currents.

A large database of information about wildlife in coastal areas was used to create Environmental Sensitivity Index maps. These maps show responders where wildlife species, sensitive shorelines, and public beaches are located. These tools help responders understand the extent of an oil spill, predict its behavior, and quickly come up with a plan for cleaning it up.

FIVE

OIL SPILL RESPONSE AND PREVENTION

The results of an oil spill can be severe and long lasting. The main goal in cleaning up an oil spill is to reduce damage to the environment. When oil spills on land, the first step is to stop the oil from reaching water. Once in water, oil has a higher movement rate and can spread much more quickly. Response workers set up barriers called berms that stop the oil from flowing. Berms can be made of soil or of synthetic materials like PVC, a type of plastic. Response workers also dig trenches to contain the oil.

If soil is contaminated, it is treated in a process known as bioremediation. Bioremediation is the technique of breaking down contaminants, including

Response workers must work quickly to prevent oil spills from causing more damage.

oil, through natural processes. Responders introduce plants, bacteria, and fungi to the contaminated soil. These introduced organisms use the oil as an energy source, turning a toxic chemical into a less toxic or harmless byproduct. However, sometimes soil conditions are not right for bioremediation. For bioremediation to be effective, the soil must have the right nutrients, moisture content, and temperature to support the degrading organisms. When these conditions are not present at the contamination site, the soil has to be excavated and moved elsewhere. The contaminated soil is stored while bioremediation takes place. When the soil is clean, it is put back.

CONTROLLED BURNS

Responders can burn oil spilled in deep water to remove it. Responders first contain the oil behind fire-resistant booms, and then they ignite it. Helicopters drop an incendiary substance, a substance designed to start fires, and ignite it with propane jets as it falls. Responders can also ignite the oil with flares, blowtorches, or an improvised incendiary device. Under normal conditions, controlled burns can remove 90 to 99 percent of the oil contained within the fire booms.

CLEANING UP THE WATER

Oil that spills in the water is particularly difficult to clean up. Booms, which work like floating fences, temporarily stop oil from

spreading on water. Containment booms can be used to surround and contain an oil slick or to block oil from reaching a sensitive area, such as wetlands. Sorbent booms absorb oil from surface water. Once booms have contained the oil slick, machines called skimmers collect the oil and pump it into a storage tank on a ship. In deep water far from inhabited areas, oil might be burned rather than collected. Fire booms are used to contain oil in one area so it can be burned.

Chemicals called dispersants also are used to remove oil from the water's surface. These chemicals break up the oil into tiny droplets that can mix more easily into the water. Tiny underwater organisms eat the droplets. This process is called biodegradation. Biodegradation is similar to bioremediation, but in bioremediation responders have to introduce the organisms that break down the hydrocarbons in oil into the environment. Biodegradation relies on organisms that are already present in the water or soil. Biodegradation breaks down oil into nontoxic compounds. Oil-eating organisms are more active in warm water than in cold water, so the rate

Many people in the Gulf region protested against British Petroleum (BP), the company that operated the *Deepwater Horizon*.

of biodegradation depends on the water temperature where the oil spill occurred.

SAVING WILDLIFE

Responders also collect wildlife impacted by oil spills. Wildlife experts clean live animals, nurse them back to health, and finally release them into new environments.

Because oil can last a long time in marshes and on beaches, oil spill cleanup activities can go on for years. It is important to prevent oil spills before they happen.

Old rigs, tankers, blowout preventers, pipelines, and refineries need to be kept in good shape. The United States and other countries now have many new rules because of past spills to prevent future spills. To get offshore drilling permits, oil companies must prove they are following the new rules.

As long as people continue to use oil and drill for oil, there will be a risk of future oil spills. To provide electricity, more and more communities have reduced their consumption of oil and other fossil fuels, turning to alternative sources of energy, such as wind and solar. But for now, most of the world runs on oil.

CASE STUDY

CHEMICAL DISPERSANTS IN THE GULF

After the *Deepwater Horizon* spill, dispersants were applied to keep oil from reaching sensitive shorelines and to reduce the impact on wildlife. Scientists also believed dispersants could increase the rate of oil biodegradation.

Dispersants first were sprayed on the oil slick from planes and boats. Then, responders predicted that applying dispersants at the underwater leak would be more effective. They developed an experimental plan.

Once the underwater plan was approved, 15,000 gallons (56,800 L) of dispersants per day were pumped down to the leaking well. This method helped prevent large oil slicks from forming at the water's surface.

Measurements showed bacteria helped consume 200,000 tons (181,000 metric tons) of oil and gas, but some scientists have been skeptical of these claims. More research is needed on the relationship between dispersants and biodegradation.

TOP TEN WORST OIL SPILLS

1. **PERSIAN GULF, 1991**

   The largest oil spill in history was purposely planned. During the 1991 Gulf War, the Iraqi military destroyed refineries, terminals, and tanker ships in Kuwait, spilling up to 336 million gallons (1.3 billion L) beginning in January.

2. ***DEEPWATER HORIZON*/MACONDO WELL, 2010**

   This oil spill in April was caused by a blowout of the Macondo Well. The blowout led to explosions that destroyed the *Deepwater Horizon* oil rig. Approximately 171 million gallons (647 million L) were spilled into the Gulf of Mexico.

3. **IXTOC 1 WELL, 1979**

   A blowout in this 2-mile (3-km) deep well caused a spill in the Bay of Campeche, Mexico. Approximately 140 million gallons (530 million L) were spilled in June.

4. **FERGANA VALLEY WELL, 1992**

   The heavily populated Fergana Valley, an industrial and agricultural area in Uzbekistan, was affected by this well blowout. Approximately 88 million gallons (333 million L) of oil were spilled in March.

5. *ATLANTIC EMPRESS/AEGEAN CAPTAIN* TANKER COLLISION, 1979

A tropical storm caused these two supertankers to collide in the Caribbean Sea off the island of Tobago in July. Explosions and fires killed 26 sailors. About 88 million gallons (333 million L) of oil spilled into the sea.

6. NOWRUZ OIL FIELD, 1983

A well in this Iranian oil field blew out and began spilling oil into the Persian Gulf in February. The Iraqi army also attacked the oil field one month later. In total, about 80 million gallons (303 million L) of oil were spilled.

7. *CASTILLO DE BELLVER*, 1983

This Spanish oil tanker caught fire off the coast of South Africa in August. It spilled 78.5 million gallons (297 million L) of oil.

8. *AMOCO CADIZ*, 1978

In March, this tanker ran aground off the coast of France, spilling its entire cargo of 68.7 million gallons (260 million L) of oil into the North Atlantic Ocean.

9. *ODYSSEY*, 1988

The *Odyssey* was a British tanker that broke apart during a severe storm in November 1988. Approximately 43.1 million gallons (163 million L) of oil were spilled about 700 miles (1,127 km) east of Nova Scotia, Canada.

10. D-103, 1980

This Libyan production well blew out in August, resulting in the release of 42 million gallons (159 million L) of oil.

GLOSSARY

CHEMICALS: Substances made up of one or more elements.

FLAMMABLE: Capable of being easily set on fire and of burning rapidly.

HABITATS: The places where plants and animals normally live.

HYDROCARBONS: Compounds containing only carbon and hydrogen.

OFFSHORE: Something located in the water.

OIL SLICK: A layer of oil floating on the surface of a body of water.

PETROLEUM: An oily, flammable liquid obtained from wells drilled in the ground.

PORE PRESSURE: The pressure of fluids in a reservoir.

RESERVOIRS: Places where things are stored or have naturally collected.

SEDIMENT: Particles that settle at the bottom of a body of water.

TOURISM: The business of encouraging travel and serving travelers.

TOXIC: Things that are poisonous.

FURTHER INFORMATION

BOOKS

Brennan, Linda Crotta. *The Gulf Oil Spill*. Minneapolis: Abdo Publishing, 2013.

Dils, Tracey E. *Oil Spill Cleaner*. Tarrytown, NY: Marshall Cavendish Benchmark, 2011.

Marrin, Albert. *Black Gold: The Story of Oil in Our Lives*. New York: Alfred A. Knopf, 2012.

Robertson, Chase. *Examining Oil and Coal*. Minneapolis: The Oliver Press, 2013.

WEBSITES

http://science.howstuffworks.com/environmental/green-science/cleaning-oil-spill.htm
Learn more about how scientists clean up spilled oil and save wildlife.

http://education.nationalgeographic.com/education/collections/oil-spills/?ar_a=1
This website features photos, videos, and activities to help you learn more about oil spills and their consequences.

INDEX